2021 ENERGY POLICY OF THE ASIAN DEVELOPMENT BANK

SUPPORTING LOW-CARBON TRANSITION IN ASIA AND THE PACIFIC

JUNE 2023

ADB

ASIAN DEVELOPMENT BANK

Note:
In this publication, "$" refers to United States dollars.

Cover design by Mike Cortes.
On the cover: **ADB Energy Policy.** The Sri Lanka Wind Power Generation Project in Thambapavani Wind Farm, Mannar, Sri Lanka will help increase access to clean and reliable power (photo by Ceylon Electricity Board).

All photos by ADB unless otherwise indicated.

Printed on recycled paper

Contents

Tables

Foreword

On 21 October 2021, the new Energy Policy of the Asian Development Bank (ADB) was approved, charting the path for energy sector operations along the aspirations of Strategy 2030 more clearly while also aligning these with the global commitments under the Paris Agreement and the Sustainable Development Goals.

The 2021 Energy Policy comes at an opportune time when the world faces what could be considered the greatest challenge humanity needs to overcome—the battle against climate change, which could either be won or lost in Asia and the Pacific. The region contributes more than half of the global greenhouse gas emissions as most of its economies have just in recent history picked up on their respective growth trajectories. It also stands to be most at risk of the drastic effects of climate change. While at the crux of the climate conundrum, the region can be well poised to disengage economic growth from rising emissions, if it plays its cards well. This is where the 2021 Energy Policy of ADB strives to find its place in supporting its developing member countries in their bid to bring the region to net-zero emissions by 2050.

There are Five Principles Set Forth by the 2021 Energy Policy to Guide ADB Energy Operations along this Path to Net-Zero:

(i)   securing energy for a prosperous and inclusive Asia and the Pacific;
(ii)   building a sustainable and resilient energy future;
(iii) supporting institutions, private sector participation, and good governance;
(iv)   promoting regional cooperation and integration; and,
(v)   integrated cross-sector operations to maximize development impact.

These principles are clear in their intent of pursuing the age-old goal of energy access for all, including the 150 million people in Asia and the Pacific without access to electricity. They speak of securing energy without having to compromise on sustainability and resilience. These objectives can only be achieved if everyone will work together and ensure that no one is left behind in the energy transformation.

We hope the 2021 Energy Policy will be continually reviewed and updated to not only guide operations but also be informed by practice as ADB continues to remain responsive and relevant for its developing member countries.

BRUNO CARRASCO
Director General concurrently Chief Compliance Officer
Sustainable Development and Climate Change Department

Abbreviations

ADB	–	Asian Development Bank
CCUS	–	carbon capture, use, and storage
CO_2	–	carbon dioxide
COVID-19	–	coronavirus disease
BESS	–	battery energy storage system
DMC	–	developing member country
GHG	–	greenhouse gas
IEA	–	International Energy Agency
IED	–	Independent Evaluation Department
LNG	–	liquefied natural gas
NDC	–	nationally determined contribution
OP1–OP7	–	operational priorities 1–7 of ADB Strategy 2030
PPP	–	public–private partnership
PV	–	photovoltaic
SDG	–	Sustainable Development Goal
T&D	–	transmission and distribution

Executive Summary

The energy landscape has changed radically over the last decade. The Sustainable Development Goals (SDGs), established in 2015, the Paris Agreement on climate change (adopted in 2015), and Strategy 2030 of the Asian Development Bank (ADB), published in 2018, set ambitious targets for providing reliable energy access to all, and amplified the calls for action on climate change. While developing countries in Asia and the Pacific have made significant advances in economic development and energy modernization, much still has to be done on these agendas.

SDG7, on affordable and clean energy, sets a target of universal access to affordable, reliable, sustainable, and modern energy services for all by 2030. It has been a critical driver of energy sector development in Asia and the Pacific since 2015. ADB's operations have played a substantial role in the progress of this goal, and has contributed to economic development and improved lives throughout the region. However, development has not been uniform between and within countries. Many people still lack access to reliable and affordable energy. Much of the expansion of energy systems has relied on fossil fuels, leading to harmful climate, health, and environmental consequences. Achieving universal energy access to a reliable and affordable energy supply across the region and supporting a low-carbon transition still require mobilizing substantial efforts and resources.

The transition to better access to cleaner energy is now accelerating. Distributed systems are reaching smaller and more remote places. The region is experiencing increased deployment of established renewable generation technologies such as solar photovoltaic systems and wind farms, and the maturing of a broad range of clean energy supply systems, intelligent controls, and new types of financial and market instruments and business models. At the same time, the traditional divide between the utility-led supply side and the consumer-led demand side has begun to blur, and national energy policies and regulatory environments are becoming more complex. Overall, these advances have opened a path toward completing the provision of reliable and affordable energy for all while still meeting global climate targets.

In this context, ADB is responding to the transition of an increasingly multifaceted energy sector with a new forward-looking energy policy to guide its operations and to be mainstreamed with other bank policies and goals. Consolidating achievements, addressing emerging challenges and opportunities, and ensuring a just and equitable transition to a low-carbon future in Asia and the Pacific will require ADB's continued support for its developing member countries (DMCs) on a broad range of energy issues. The 2021 Energy Policy is fully committed to the seven operational priorities of Strategy 2030 and the global commitments that Strategy 2030 supports, including the SDGs and the Paris Agreement.

The objectives of the policy are to help DMCs accelerate the development of sustainable and resilient energy systems that provide reliable and affordable access for all, foster inclusive economic growth and social development, and support the low-carbon transition in Asia and the Pacific. The policy recognizes that the sector financing needs across the region considerably exceed the sector support provided by ADB and therefore prioritizes ADB's limited resources to tackle the most demanding energy challenges. To achieve the policy's objectives, ADB's energy sector operations will be based on the following policy principles:

Policy principle 1: ADB will support efforts to bring affordable, reliable, sustainable, and modern energy to all, so as to eradicate extreme poverty and reduce social inequalities.

Policy principle 2: ADB will provide support to its DMCs to tackle climate change, enhance environmental sustainability, and build climate and disaster resilience.

Policy principle 3: ADB will support the institutional development, financial sustainability, and good governance of energy sector institutions and companies, as well as private sector participation. It will also help create the policy frameworks needed to manage the energy transition.

Policy principle 4: ADB will promote regional energy cooperation and the integration of energy systems to strengthen energy security and increase cross-border access to cleaner energy sources.

Policy principle 5: ADB will continue to combine finance, knowledge, partnerships, and its country-focused approach to deliver integrated solutions with comprehensive and magnified development impacts.

ADB will work to accelerate the provision of energy for all as well as the low-carbon transition through the deployment and transfer of a wide range of technological innovations. It will promote the adoption of distributed systems and mini-grids to reach underserved areas. ADB will pursue the dual approach of reducing the carbon intensity of electricity generation and increasing the share of electricity in the total final energy consumption. In addition, new digital technologies and energy storage systems can substantially increase energy efficiency. ADB will also promote the adoption of technologies such as advanced biofuels; geothermal systems; demonstrations of ocean energy; and carbon capture, use, and storage projects unless they are connected to enhanced oil recovery. Large hydropower systems and waste-to-energy plants may be supported after careful consideration of their political, social, and environmental contexts.

ADB is aware that the energy transition will require both additional financing and a well-sequenced plan for decarbonization. Natural gas can, under some conditions, offer a lower-carbon alternative to more polluting fuels—such as coal and oil in power and heat generation—and provide flexible resources to allow more renewable energy to be integrated into the grid. However, concerns have also been raised about whether the continued use of natural gas is compatible with climate stabilization goals. Therefore, ADB will offer limited and conditional support to natural gas projects.

Since coal is a main source of greenhouse gases and air pollution in the Asia and Pacific region and is increasingly at odds with the long-term environmental plans of DMCs, ADB will focus its support to renewable and low-carbon solutions and confirm its current practice of not financing new coal-based capacity for power and heat. ADB will also support the early retirement and decommissioning of coal resources to help DMCs achieve a planned phaseout of coal in the Asia and Pacific region.

The transition to a carbon-neutral economy will affect every aspect of how DMCs produce goods and provide services, but it also offers new opportunities. It will considerably affect workers and communities, as well as future jobs and demand for skills. Planning for a just transition will be critical in managing this process. The aim is to mitigate negative socioeconomic impacts and increase opportunities associated with the transition; support affected workers and communities; and enhance access to sustainable, inclusive, and resilient livelihoods for all. ADB will therefore work with DMCs to support planning and technology transfers in a way that involves all relevant stakeholders and affected groups at all stages, so as to achieve a just energy transition.

ADB will conduct its energy sector operations in line with its environmental and social safeguard policies and the principles of justice, equity, diversity, and inclusiveness. Gender equality and women's increased leadership in the public and private energy sectors will continue to be important goals in its operations. ADB also recognizes its duty to inform and engage with local populations during the planning and implementation of projects, since their lives may be affected. It is essential that the potential benefits for and impacts on all disadvantaged and vulnerable groups are carefully considered during the planning and implementation of these projects.

The energy policy principles will be implemented in each DMC through ADB's country partnership strategies, which are the primary platform for agreeing on priorities and delivering operational programs at the country level. In accordance with Strategy 2030, and in recognition of the significant diversity across DMCs, ADB will adopt differentiated approaches in line with each DMC's level of economic development, resource endowment, and nationally determined low-carbon transition pathways. ADB is also mindful of the principle of common but differentiated responsibilities set out for the Parties to the Paris Agreement, which allows countries to reflect their unique circumstances as they plan to achieve global peaking of greenhouse gas emissions and carbon neutrality as soon as possible.

ADB realizes that the policy objectives require additional concessional financing and technology transfers, as well as financing for infrastructure investments. ADB will help develop capital markets and make available its full range of financial instruments—including grants and sovereign and nonsovereign loans across the range of modalities, such as green bonds, credit enhancements and guarantees, and private sector equity. It will also continue to engage in policy dialogue and provide technical assistance and knowledge solutions. ADB will partner with other development institutions in all these areas to improve coordination and leverage impact.

Implementing these policies will also require robust long-term planning, improved governance, favorable policy environments, more efficient institutions, and better service delivery by public and private operators. ADB will therefore make available all the tools of its multidimensional support and continue to promote institutional development, policy reforms, and regional energy cooperation through integrated approaches with knowledge sharing, technical advice, and capacity building.

Energy sector operations play a vital role in achieving ADB's vision of a prosperous, resilient, inclusive, and sustainable Asia and the Pacific. Accordingly, this policy applies to all of ADB's sovereign and nonsovereign operations, including project loans, sector loans, policy-based loans, results-based loans, financial intermediary loans, equity participation, and technical assistance. The 2021 Energy Policy provides ADB with the priorities and guidance to support the DMCs in meeting their ever-evolving development needs.

I. Introduction

Expanded energy access and increased security of energy supply have contributed to economic development and better quality of life across the Asia and Pacific region. The energy operations of the Asian Development Bank (ADB) have made substantial contributions to the energy sector's growth and hold a significant share of ADB's overall operations, averaging about 21% of total approved lending to developing member countries (DMCs) from 2009 to 2020. Over that period, ADB's lending and grants in the sector totaled $42.5 billion, of which about 23% were nonsovereign operations.

The Sustainable Development Goal (SDG) on affordable and clean energy (SDG7) set a target of universal access to affordable, reliable, and modern energy services by 2030. Energy sector growth has not, however, been uniform across and within countries, and the expansion of energy systems came at the cost of harmful climate and environmental consequences. Achieving universal energy access and sufficient energy supply across the region and supporting a low-carbon transition still requires mobilizing substantial efforts and resources. The SDGs also called for a "Decade of Action," such as the rapid implementation of sustainable solutions to the challenges relating to poverty, climate change, gender, inequality, and financing gaps.

The 2021 Energy Policy is an update to the 2009 Energy Policy to guide ADB's energy sector operations. It focuses on energy operations that are optimally aligned with ADB's Strategy 2030[1] and the global commitments that Strategy 2030 supports, including the SDGs, the related Financing for Development Agenda,[2] and the Paris Agreement[3] on climate change (Paris Agreement).

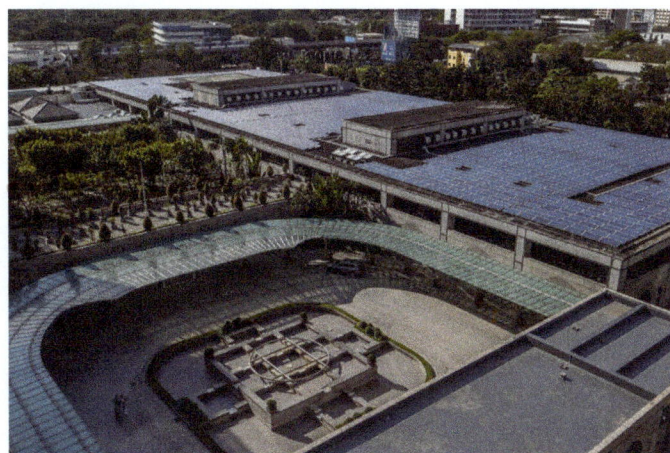

ADB Headquarters. Drone photograph of the ADB's solar panels.

The policy also responds to the findings of ADB's Independent Evaluation Department (IED) in its assessment of the ADB Energy Policy and Program, 2009–2019, which evaluated the alignment of the 2009 Energy Policy with Strategy 2030 and recent changes in the energy sector landscape.[4] In addition, this publication proposes that ADB regularly review and refine its approach to energy operations so that it can better respond to the evolving needs of DMCs and use the best options to meet those needs.

---

[1] ADB. 2018. *Strategy 2030: Achieving a Prosperous, Inclusive, Resilient, and Sustainable Asia and the Pacific.* Manila.
[2] United Nations (UN). Financing for Sustainable Development.
[3] UN. The Paris Agreement.
[4] ADB. 2020. *Sector-Wide Evaluation: ADB Energy Policy and Program, 2009–2019.* Manila.

II. Energy Sector Issues

The main challenges for DMCs in the energy sector still lie in ensuring (i) universal access to electricity, and clean cooking and heating options for all households; (ii) energy security to support economic growth; (iii) sustainability across the dimensions of financial viability, effective operation and maintenance of infrastructure, resilience to climate change and extreme events, climate mitigation via lower-carbon use, health, and environmental impacts; and (iv) sector governance, including regulations, utilities' performance, and private sector participation. While many DMCs have made significant progress in these areas, they need continued support in consolidating achievements and addressing emerging challenges and opportunities.

A. Energy Access

Progress on access to energy has been rapid across developing Asia and the Pacific, reaching an overall electrification rate of 96% in 2019, or a 16% increase since 2010. However, the electrification rates of individual DMCs vary widely and many power systems continue to be hampered by unreliable supply. Currently, about 940 million people in Asia and the Pacific still experience frequent interruptions, about 350 million people do not enjoy adequate supply, and about 150 million people still have no access to electricity.[5] The issue of how to achieve adequate, reliable, and affordable universal access will therefore remain on the agendas of governments as well as national and international development financing institutions.

Many, but not all DMCs have accelerated energy access through grid extensions, and the focus in those countries has now shifted to reaching remote areas through off-grid solutions such as mini-grids. However, the financial sustainability of mini-grids and their affordability for consumers remain major challenges because sustainable business models are yet to emerge. With new technology and growing private sector interest, the service provided by mini-grids may become more reliable for lighting and home appliances, and sufficient to support productive end uses such as water pumping and agricultural processing. New technology options, especially cheaper battery storage, will accelerate the adoption of off-grid solutions.

---

[5] International Energy Agency (IEA). 2020. World Energy Outlook 2020: Access to Electricity Database (accessed 10 August 2021).

Town Electrification Investment Program in Papua New Guinea. Julie Andreas, a community member in Buvussi Village, received electricity a week earlier after living in her house for 42 years.

Access to clean fuels and technologies for cooking and heating remains a challenge for DMCs in both rural and urban contexts. Cooking with traditional fuels such as wood, charcoal, and animal manure is a major source of indoor air pollution and associated health problems. Every year, 3.8 million people die prematurely from illnesses (e.g., pneumonia, stroke, ischemic heart disease, chronic obstructive pulmonary disease, and lung cancer) attributable to the household air pollution caused by inefficient use of solid fuels and kerosene for cooking.[6] Since these impacts disproportionately burden women and children, lack of access to sustainable cooking solutions is also a social problem. In addition, using charcoal and wood to cook has a significant impact on climate change, contributing 3% of global carbon dioxide (CO_2) emissions every year. DMCs are not on track to meet the target of universal access to clean cooking by 2030 because 1.6 billion people still have no such access. This represents 43% of the population in the region.[7] These challenges must be confronted during the 2020s. In addition to electricity, biogas, liquefied petroleum gas, and natural gas, this decade will likely bring new advanced biomass cookstove models, solar cookers, collectors, and disks for cooking and heating applications.

Energy services enabled by modern technologies in both rural and urban environments have a major impact on people's daily lives. Progress on energy access has increased household income and consumption, children's study time and years of schooling, and men and women's time spent working. However, persistent and widespread unequal access to energy services makes it imperative to prioritize support to all disadvantaged and vulnerable groups—women, poor people, racial and ethnic minorities, indigenous peoples, people with disabilities, older persons, and other marginalized people. Women in rural areas are particularly and disproportionally affected by the lack of access to clean and modern energy services. Achieving energy access in an equitable manner therefore still requires mobilizing substantial efforts and resources.

---

6   World Health Organization. 2018. *Household Air Pollution and Health.*
7   IEA. 2019. World Energy Outlook 2019: Access to Clean Cooking Database (accessed 10 August 2021).

Moreover, the coronavirus disease (COVID-19) pandemic has created a risk of reversing the current level of progress. It highlighted the critical need for electricity access to support related necessities such as health care and hospitals. Access to reliable electricity is also an essential requirement for the transportation, distribution, and storage of vaccines, which will be instrumental in ending the COVID-19 crisis.

B.   Energy Security

In addition to energy access, DMCs need to ensure energy security to support continued economic expansion and meet demand from population growth and urbanization. The population of the Asia and Pacific region increased by 1.7% per annum from 1990 to 2019, and urbanization accelerated from 36% in 1990 to 51% in 2019. The region's gross domestic product, in constant prices, has grown on average 6% per annum from 1990 to 2019, while its primary energy supply increased by about 4% per annum in the same period.[8]

In 2019, coal accounted for 36% of the primary energy supply in the region; followed by oil at 23%; renewable energy such as hydro, wind, solar, geothermal, and biomass at 20%; natural gas at 16%; and nuclear at 5%. Although fossil fuels are still dominant at a combined 75%, they have fallen from a share of 87% in 2009, while the share of renewable energy has doubled from 10% since that year.

Continuing economic growth and urbanization will require the development of affordable and reliable energy systems with substantial additional electricity-generating capacity, and flexible power systems that can balance fluctuations in demand and supply. Given the current aspirations of DMCs toward much lower emissions, the policy has used the sustainable development scenario of the International Energy Agency (IEA) as a basis—it assumes ambitious national clean energy policies and investments that ADB can support to meet sustainable energy objectives, such as energy access, the Paris Agreement, and air quality goals. Based on that IEA scenario, installed electricity-generating capacity would increase by about 7% per annum, from 3,386 gigawatts in 2019 to 6,113 gigawatts in 2030. In particular, the capacity of solar, wind, and hydropower will grow at a rate of 11% per annum (footnote 5). Accordingly, and with sufficient ambition and international support, the Asia and Pacific region's investments in renewable energy generation by 2030 could reach $1.3 trillion per annum, doubling the amount from the previous decade.[9]

Such a rapid expansion of renewable energy capacity would require strong, resilient, and flexible transmission and distribution (T&D) systems that allow the DMCs to increase reliability; manage variability; balance network capabilities across appropriate geographic scales, including cross-border interconnections; and adopt appropriate grid management solutions, such as digitalization and storage technologies. Current investments in the region's electricity grid systems—including T&D and energy storage—are estimated to total about $1 trillion per annum.

---

[8]   United Nations Economic and Social Commission for Asia and the Pacific (UNESCAP). 2021. Asia Pacific Energy Portal. Bangkok (accessed 4 May 2022).
[9]   Wood Mackenzie projection released in June 2021.

Improved end-use energy efficiency can play a key role in reducing energy demand. It can also lower the costs of energy transition, since it normally costs less to deploy proven energy efficiency measures than add new supply or generation capacity. Energy efficiency can result in greater economic productivity and provide social and environmental benefits such as increased energy affordability, less infrastructure construction, improved air quality, reduced pollution, and global climate change mitigation. Energy intensity has steadily declined across Asia and the Pacific, and efficiency gains in the region have outpaced the global rate of progress. Still, the region's energy intensity remains higher than the global average, and the potential for the application of energy efficiency measures is large.[10]

Accelerating progress on energy efficiency gains across the region could contribute to the agendas of energy security and energy access while also producing cost and environmental benefits. Clear policies and the right incentive structure for expanding demand-side energy efficiency are needed to fully capture the potential. Many of the region's large DMCs have taken measures to systematically address energy efficiency in their policies and regulation, but these efforts are not replicated across all DMCs. In addition to policies that promote and reward energy efficiency, it takes innovative financing mechanisms and more private sector investment to expedite region-wide efficiency gains.

C.   Environmental Sustainability

Strategy 2030 stresses that ADB's vision of a prosperous, inclusive, resilient, and sustainable Asia and the Pacific hinges on the success of the region in tackling climate change, enhancing environmental sustainability, and building climate and disaster resilience. ADB's Climate Change Operational Framework sets out how ADB will support increased resilience and enhanced mitigation.[11] Asia and the Pacific share the same atmosphere with all other countries as a global public good. While DMCs did not contribute the majority of historic emissions that have led to the current climate crisis, their emissions are now significant, and they are among the most vulnerable to the effects of the crisis. If the current trajectory is not reversed, Asia and the Pacific will suffer more than most other regions from the impacts of climate change, air pollution, and biodiversity loss.

Coal and other fossil fuels have played a large part in providing access to energy in Asia and the Pacific and enabling its economic development. But their use harms the environment and accelerates climate change. In 2019, about 50% of global CO_2 emissions from fossil fuel (coal, oil, and natural gas) combustion was from Asia and the Pacific (footnote 5). Consequently, the energy sector of Asia and the Pacific is a critical area for a direct and effective response to climate change, and for building climate and disaster resilience. ADB's deep and long engagement in this sector means that it is uniquely placed to play a pivotal role.

---

[10]   UNESCAP. 2021. *2021 Regional Trends Report: Shaping a Sustainable Energy Future in Asia and the Pacific.* Bangkok. (February).

[11]   ADB. 2017. *Climate Change Operational Framework 2017–2030: Enhanced Action for Low Greenhouse-Gas Emissions and Climate-Resilient Development.* Manila.

Although the Asia and Pacific region's contribution to global greenhouse gas (GHG) emissions is high, its per capita CO_2 emissions are currently about 4.1 tons per year, well below the 8.8 tons per capita average in Organisation for Economic Co-operation and Development countries, reflecting relatively low per capita energy consumption.[12] With continued economic growth and increases in population and wealth, per capita emissions from the region are expected to augment if energy systems continue to rely on the expanded use of fossil fuels. The combustion of fossil fuels is also the main source of local air pollutants that cause immediate and lasting harm to public health and ecosystem services. Some of the most polluted cities in the world in terms of annual average particulate concentration are in Asia and the Pacific.

Climate change contributes to an increased frequency and intensity of extreme weather events and associated risks. Many DMCs are highly exposed and vulnerable to resulting natural hazards such as sea level rise, changes in rainfall patterns, cyclones, floods, landslides, droughts, and heat waves. Pacific countries and other small island states, as well as some areas in South Asia, are the first to encounter the impacts of rising sea levels because of warming trends. DMCs are suffering losses from disasters because of insufficient regard for climate and disaster risk in the design and location of infrastructure. The impact of climate change and the disruption of ecosystems can severely impair livelihoods and food security, which in turn can undermine human health.

To enhance disaster resilience in the energy sector, many advanced economies in the region developed high levels of grid redundancy, for example, or shifted from overhead lines to underground cabling. Such measures are costly and may seem unaffordable for DMCs whose priorities are to extend service to unserved areas or strengthen the grid to tackle serious service deficits. However, not investing in resilience measures can lead to higher life-cycle costs because of infrastructure failure and rebuilding needs after extreme events.

D.   Sector Governance

Accommodating greater flexibility and new technologies will require governance, market, and regulatory reforms in many DMCs. Many of the region's electricity market systems and their supporting regulations were developed based on a traditional, centralized system not designed to deal with the supply-side variability that comes from intermittent renewable sources. They were also not designed to accommodate a large role of renewable energy, which is characterized by high capital costs but extremely low operating costs, the deployment of distributed energy resources, and demand-side participation in the operation of the power system. The region's governments continue to deregulate and reform their power subsectors to increase efficiency, and restructure state-owned utilities to allow competition. New power exchanges are likely to emerge, and existing ones are likely to be strengthened. Newer power generation technologies and fuels are being placed on a more equal footing with fossil fuels, particularly by pricing the social and environmental costs of fossil-fuel use through mechanisms such as carbon taxes, emission-trading systems, and international offset mechanisms. However, cost-reflective tariffs and

---

[12]   World Bank. World Bank Open Data. CO_2 Emissions (metric ton per capita) (accessed 2 July 2021).

governance measures to ensure sector accountability and sustainability remain an issue in many countries in the region.

Subsidies have long been used in the energy sector to promote desired objectives. There are pros and cons to subsidies. Subsidies can help the transition to cleaner energy. However, they can also induce unwanted distortions in the economy. They have been used traditionally to ensure the affordability of energy services, and transport fuels were subsidized to ensure economic productivity, mobility, and quality of life. More recently, subsidies have been used to accelerate the deployment of renewable energy. Fossil-fuel subsidies are typically concentrated in upstream wholesale energy production and distribution operations such as coal mining and petroleum fuel supply, while renewable energy subsidies are typically concentrated at the project level and retail end of the supply chain, such as rooftop solar. Financial incentives in the form of feed-in tariffs for renewable energy are now being eliminated or reduced as renewable energy has become more competitive. To avoid unwanted market distortions and promote economic efficiency, energy subsidies should be targeted, time-bound, and transparent across the full spectrum of fuel types and energy services.

Energy subsidies also help governments maintain regulated low prices in domestic markets, partly to protect consumers from swings in international fuel prices or the changing economic value of domestic fuels. Subsidies can include direct payments to fuel companies, tax exemptions, subsidized credit, provision of underpriced public services, and support to energy companies using state budgets. Subsidization and cross-subsidization can also occur through differentiated electricity tariffs applied to large corporations and household consumers. Energy subsidies create intentional market distortions that can increase access for poor people but can also hamper investments in renewable energy and energy efficiency, as well as the transition to sustainable energy systems. Furthermore, untargeted subsidies disproportionately benefit the wealthier sections of the population, who consume substantially more fuels and electricity than an average consumer. Targeting subsidies to achieve their objectives without unintended consequences remains an important policy challenge in the region.

As the Asia and Pacific region recovers from COVID-19, improving the resilience and security of the energy sector has been clearly identified as a priority. Institutional capacity building remains an important factor in achieving good governance. Although most, but not all, energy systems have operated well so far, their typical reliance on imported expertise, technologies, and fossil fuels makes them vulnerable. Renewable energy technologies, when manufactured, deployed, and maintained locally, have the potential to create a resilient energy generation source that uses indigenous resources. While COVID-19 has reduced the cost of imported fossil fuels because of lower demand, any future crisis could limit DMCs' access to fossil fuels or drive up fossil fuel prices. Therefore, a reduction in the use of imported fuel augments the potential resilience of the energy systems of DMCs. Moreover, the increased use of information and communication technologies in energy infrastructure will require a focus on cybersecurity to avoid security threats.

Given the scale of investment requirements of around $800 billion per year, energy sector reforms in DMCs should lead to more opportunities for private sector participation, particularly in the subsector of electricity generation.[13] While a fully open subsector with a competitive electricity market is still a rarity in the region, many DMCs have enabled private sector investments via regulated entry points such as public–private partnerships (PPPs), renewable energy auctions, and independent power producers with long-term power purchase agreements. ADB will continue to work to mobilize higher levels of concessional financing and private sector investments, increase technical support, and focus on catalytic activities, innovations, and affordable transfer of green technologies.

E.   Changing Energy Landscape

The energy transition to cleaner and more sustainable systems has already begun, and significant declines in the costs of renewable energy technologies are accelerating this transition. Between 2010 and 2019, the costs of solar photovoltaic (PV) systems decreased by 82%, while those of concentrating solar power plants fell by 47%, followed by onshore (39%) and offshore (29%) wind farms.[14] These trends, which are projected to continue, led to a reduction in the cost differential between traditional fossil-fuel power generation technologies and renewable energy generators. The cost of electricity from unsubsidized renewable energy can be lower than that from new conventional generators, and, in some cases, renewable power costs are competitive with those of existing conventional generators.[15] The development of ultra-high-voltage technology for both alternating and direct current electricity transmission, together with rapidly declining costs for solar and wind power, have increased the feasibility of large-scale development and the use of hydro, wind, and solar resources in remote and inter-subregional contexts. However, the intermittent nature of solar and wind energy sources also means that grid-scale storage and alternative generation capacity are required to integrate them effectively.

In addition to cost declines for established technologies, newer technologies are maturing that can contribute to a clean energy transition. Battery energy storage systems (BESSs) have experienced cost reductions and performance improvements, amplifying their relevance in managing variable renewable generation. Electrification; carbon capture, use, and storage (CCUS); green hydrogen (hydrogen made without fossil fuels); and advanced biofuels can all play a role in transitioning the business areas that are more difficult to decarbonize, such as long-range transport, industry, and space cooling and heating. Battery electric vehicles, plug-in hybrid technologies, and fuel cell systems enable the transport sector to move away from fossil fuels. In industries, direct electric heating, electric arcs, and induction heating offer opportunities to electrify processes that require high temperatures. Heat pumps can provide efficient heating for industries as well as space heating and cooling, even in a context of generation sources with low heat content.

Natural gas has historically been seen as an important alternative in reducing emissions from coal and balancing variable renewable generation. Concerns have been raised about whether the continued use of natural gas is compatible with climate stabilization goals. Replacing coal with natural gas reduces but does not eliminate GHG emissions, and fugitive emissions from natural gas production and transmission may be responsible

---

[13]   ADB. 2017. *Meeting Asia's Infrastructure Needs.* Manila.
[14]   International Renewable Energy Agency (IRENA). 2020. *Renewable Power Generation Costs in 2019.* Abu Dhabi.
[15]   Lazard. 2020. *Levelized Cost of Energy, Levelized Cost of Storage, and Levelized Cost of Hydrogen 2020.*

for a meaningful share of global methane and nitrogen emissions. Currently, natural gas is used across the Asia and Pacific region in buildings, industry, and power generation, including combined heat and power plants. The region imports 9% of the world's total pipeline imports of gas and 75% of liquefied natural gas (LNG). LNG terminals and gas T&D infrastructure require large capital investments. To maximize the value of these investments, it is likely that many of the region's economies will continue to include gas in their energy transition strategies to replace coal and fuel oil. Accordingly, current supply contracts and gas deployment plans suggest that the use of natural gas will increase in the region until at least 2030.

International bodies and developing countries have analyzed the pathways to carbon neutrality in light of the recent technology developments and cost declines. Reaching neutrality by about 2050 would require extensive efforts in the energy sector, including (i) rapid transition of power systems to renewable energy, (ii) greater use of electricity in industry and transport, (iii) application of CCUS solutions to remaining coal and natural gas operations, (iv) increased use of hydrogen and hydrogen-derived synthetic fuels, and (v) wider use of sustainable alternative fuels and feedstock such as bioenergy.[16]

Such a course of action not only includes replacing fossil fuels with renewable energy sources in electricity production but also electricity replacing fossil fuels as an energy carrier in the final energy consumption. These two aspects of the transition require changes in both the energy sector and in end-user systems. Also, along with increased investments in renewable electricity, improvements in power systems are necessary so that they can integrate variable renewable electricity sources, as is strengthening the infrastructure to cope with more electricity demand.

To ensure that the next phase of growth across the region is sustainable, economic development should become less energy intensive and more dependent on cleaner sources. Moreover, infrastructure investment should be planned along a time horizon that meets the needs of the present generation without compromising the ability of future generations to meet their own needs.

---

[16] IEA. 2020. *Energy Technology Perspectives 2020*. Paris.

III. Lessons

A. Lessons from Evaluation

During 2009–2020, ADB approved $42.5 billion in financing for the energy sector, making it the second-largest sector in terms of volume of ADB support, after transport. Total approvals in the electricity T&D subsector accounted for 39% of the total portfolio during this period, followed by renewable energy projects at 21%, conventional generation projects (mostly combined-cycle gas-fired power plants) at 14%, sector reforms and institutional strengthening at 15%, and energy efficiency and conservation at 11%.

In 2020, IED comprehensively reviewed ADB's 2009 Energy Policy[17] and its energy operations during 2009–2019 (footnote 4). The IED evaluation considered the profound changes in the energy landscape over that period, and the new priorities set out in Strategy 2030. It highlighted significant successes in ADB's energy sector operations, and found that the 2009 Energy Policy had been relevant to the ADB program during the reviewed period. However, IED also determined that it was no longer adequately aligned with the global consensus on climate change, the ongoing global transformation of the energy sector, gender equality goals, and recent changes in the energy sectors of DMCs. When the 2009 Energy Policy was adopted, its objectives were aligned with the needs of the energy sectors in DMCs, Strategy 2020, approaches of other multilateral development banks, and climate change priorities at that time. However, the Paris Agreement of 2015, the SDGs, recent technological developments, and Strategy 2030 have created new conditions and demands for ADB's energy assistance. Although ADB has not financed investments in coal-fired power plants since 2013, even though the 2009 Energy Policy allowed such financing, the current energy and climate change contexts present the opportunity and rationale to support the phaseout of coal-fired power plants in the region. IED recommended an update that considers the opportunities provided by innovative technologies, price dynamics, decentralized energy systems, digitalization, energy efficiency, and new business models for enhancing sustainability, resilience, inclusiveness, and energy access and security. It also proposed that guidance on energy sector operations be updated more frequently.

B. Stakeholder Consultations

The formulation of the new policy benefited from an extensive consultation process begun in September 2020 and continued until July 2021. More than 40 formal meetings were held with stakeholders that ranged from the governments of ADB members to civil society

---

17 ADB. 2009. *Energy Policy*. Manila.

organizations to technical experts from around the world, and many written submissions were received through a dedicated web page where drafts of the proposed policy were publicly posted. While this resulted in a huge diversity of views, it also generated widespread support for the main principles of enhanced energy access, affordability, security, and resilience; additional concessional finance and technology transfers for decarbonization; alignment with the Paris Agreement; less use of fossil fuels while maintaining reliable power supply during the energy transition; and more emphasis on a just transition for all affected people and communities.

C. Comparisons with Other Multilateral Development Banks

Other multilateral development banks have issued updated policies, strategies, or guidance notes to guide their energy sector operations. They all mandate investments in clean and efficient energy supply with a focus on environmental sustainability, an effective policy and enabling environment, greater private sector investment, and regional cooperation and integration. They vary in the degree to which options are restricted, particularly with respect to fossil fuels. Appendix 1 summarizes their approach to the energy transition, including their position on fossil fuels.

National Solar Park Project Site. This ADB-supported National Solar Power Project demonstrates the viability of developing large-scale solar photovoltaic power generation in Cambodia by mobilizing public and private resources.

IV. Overarching Considerations for Energy Operations

ADB recognizes the central role of energy in equitable and inclusive socioeconomic development and that the primary objective of its energy sector operations is to help DMCs provide universal access to reliable and affordable clean and sustainable energy. The following paragraphs elaborate the overarching aspects that were considered in the design of the new energy policy, and which will be considered in the design and execution of energy sector operations.

Multidimensional support. In accordance with Strategy 2030, the 2021 Energy Policy underscores that ADB's support to DMCs in the energy sector requires ongoing commitment to SDG7 and encourages urgent action to combat climate change and its impacts and protect environments while fostering economic growth. ADB recognizes that energy services must be affordable, reliable, and resilient for productive uses, urban populations, and rural communities. It realizes that these objectives cannot be achieved only by supporting infrastructure investments through technical assistance, grants, guarantees and other risk management instruments, and loans. Such objectives also require robust long-term planning, accelerated deployment and transfers of sustainable green technologies, improved governance, favorable policy environments, more efficient institutions, and better service delivery by public and private operators. Hence, ADB will continue to support institutional development, policy reforms, and regional energy cooperation through integrated approaches with knowledge sharing, technical advice, capacity building, and financing, consistent with the Group of Twenty (G20) Principles for Quality Infrastructure Investment to enhance efficiency, affordability, sustainability, and resilience of new energy assets.

Differentiated approach. In accordance with Strategy 2030, and in recognition of the significant diversity across DMCs, the implementation of the policy will adopt but differentiated approaches in line with each DMC's level of economic development, resource endowment, and nationally determined low-carbon transition pathways. ADB will prioritize support for essential energy access services in the poorest and most vulnerable countries, including fragile and conflict-affected situations and small island developing states, through greater use of low-carbon and renewable energy sources, and assistance for the rehabilitation of infrastructure to enhance energy security and climate resilience. Support for a just transition will also factor in resource considerations in line with this differentiated approach. In low-income and lower-middle-income countries, ADB will continue to support reforms in the energy sector, including reforms of state-owned enterprises; the development of green and inclusive energy infrastructure to enhance productivity and competitiveness; the promotion of gender equality; and greater participation of the private sector in delivering energy infrastructure and services.

Tanahu Hydropower Project in Nepal. Bishnu Bika works in a mill at her village in Manpur where electricity flows from the ADB-supported Ghiring substation in Tanaun.

ADB supports the principle of common but differentiated responsibilities and respective capabilities in light of national circumstances that is embedded in the Paris Agreement. It allows countries to reflect their unique circumstances and provides them with the necessary flexibility in the choice of their measures as they plan to achieve global peaking of GHG emissions and carbon neutrality as soon as possible. The Parties to the Paris Agreement have agreed to reflect their highest possible ambition in establishing their low-carbon pathways, recognizing that it will take longer for developing countries to reach their peak in GHG emissions. ADB will therefore support all DMCs through finance, technical assistance, policy dialogue, and knowledge sharing to increase the ambition of their national energy plans, nationally determined contributions (NDCs), and long-term climate strategies; and will encourage the low-carbon transition in the region by all means available and appropriate to national circumstances.

Inclusive energy operations. ADB will conduct its energy sector activities in line with the principles of justice, equity, diversity, and inclusiveness. In accordance with Strategy 2030's operational priority 2 (OP2), gender equality and women's increased leadership in the public and private sector are recognized as valuable goals in their own right as well as for their value in helping advance socioeconomic development. Despite progress in Asia and the Pacific, persistent gender gaps remain. Gender equality in employment, decision-making, and leadership will therefore continue to be an important goal throughout the consultation, planning, and implementation of energy sector operations.

ADB recognizes its duty to inform and engage with local populations during the planning of renewable energy and infrastructure resilience projects that will affect their lives. This process will seek to empower communities through meaningful consultation. It is essential that the potential benefits for and impacts on all disadvantaged and vulnerable groups—women, poor people, racial and ethnic minorities, indigenous peoples, people with disabilities, older persons, and other marginalized people—are carefully considered during project or program preparation and implementation. Project teams should conduct meaningful consultation with care and with an understanding of the overlapping nature of issues faced by many disadvantaged and vulnerable groups.

Energy sector processes will have a key role in determining the future impacts of climate change. Long-term changes—such as air pollution, the disruption of ecosystems, rising sea levels, and changes to rainfall patterns—will have the greatest impact on the future lives of today's children. It is therefore incumbent on ADB to ensure that children and youths also have a voice in the energy sector processes that will determine their future, and that those views are given due weight in the consultation procedures during preparation and implementation of energy projects.[18]

Concessional climate resources. The ongoing energy transformation is causing a surge in the need for energy investments in Asia and the Pacific—on top of the already high demand for infrastructure investment driven by urbanization, industrialization, and population growth. ADB will use its competitive advantage, convening power, and regional knowledge to leverage international climate finance, including international concessional resources, to help its DMCs achieve their national targets and international commitments expeditiously and to achieve a rapid shift to greener and cleaner economies. ADB will also continue to work to mobilize higher levels of concessional financing and private sector investments to support the necessary transition.

Expanding private sector participation. The private sector also has a pivotal role in filling the investment gaps. This role not only hinges on the extensive resources of private capital but also on the private sector spearheading innovation in technology and business models that support creativity, dynamism, and efficiency in the pursuit of sustainable solutions. ADB will use private sector operations and PPP resources in close collaboration with its public sector operations to provide integrated solutions to DMCs in the energy sector. Public sector operations, including project lending, policy-based lending, and technical assistance, can advance energy sector reforms and regulatory frameworks that allow the private sector to make an important contribution to the energy transition. In doing so, ADB will promote the commercial sustainability of sector utilities and companies in DMCs through high standards of corporate governance, integrity, transparency, and social and environmental safeguards.

ADB can increase project viability through project financing, PPPs, technical assistance, blended finance with concessional funds, and other instruments that bring in private sector capital from the market. Such interventions can be supplemented and their impact enhanced by mobilizing third-party concessional financing facilities that can be deployed, taking advantage of ADB's operational and sector expertise. ADB will also help structure sustainable energy projects to ensure optimal risk sharing, and provide risk management services through guarantees, interest rate hedging instruments, and other products such as credit insurance. Financial risk management instruments can bring comfort and engage the commercial finance sector in early-stage markets, and can be key to achieving investments in first-of-a-kind projects.

---

[18]   UN. 1989. *Convention on the Rights of the Child*, Treaty no. 27531. United Nations Treaty Series, 1577. Article 12.2.

An ADB strategic and operational priority is to ensure an expanded role for private sector financing and solutions to complement what is provided by ADB's sovereign operations. ADB should therefore seek to increase the volume of financing through its Private Sector Operations Department for energy projects that are aligned with this energy policy. At the same time, ADB recognizes the need to avoid crowding out other sources of private sector financing and steering investment resources away from countries with less-developed financial markets. Hence, ADB will guide its nonsovereign energy operations to expand into new markets, including challenging markets such as fragile and conflict-affected situations and small island developing states. In this context, ADB will consider smaller project sizes with potentially higher risk and development impact, including inclusive business models to achieve greater gender equality, job creation, and access to affordable clean energy for households and the productive use of energy.

Accounting for externalities. ADB incorporates the social cost of carbon across all operations, including in the energy sector. The current unit value used by ADB is based on the empirical estimates of the global social cost of carbon reported by the Intergovernmental Panel on Climate Change, to be increased annually in real terms to allow for the potentially increasing marginal damage of global warming over time.[19] This unit value is used in economic analyses to estimate the value of avoided GHG emissions for projects that reduce emissions and the cost in damage created for projects that increase emissions. The unit value will be revised in the future as more and newer estimates of damages caused by climate change become available.

---

[19]   ADB. 2017. *Guidelines for the Economic Analysis of Projects*. Manila.

V. The 2021 Energy Policy

In response to the changes in the energy sector and to reflect feedback from stakeholders, lessons from evaluations, and policy analysis, ADB has developed its new energy policy. Its objectives are to help DMCs accelerate the development of sustainable and resilient energy systems that provide reliable and affordable access to all, foster inclusive economic growth and social development, and support the low-carbon transition in Asia and the Pacific. The policy recognizes that the sector financing needs across the region considerably exceed the sector support provided by ADB and therefore prioritizes ADB's limited resources to tackle the most difficult energy challenges for which commercial financing may not be readily available. The policy seeks to ensure that DMCs can adopt modern clean energy technologies, innovative financial instruments, and new business models; and develop energy markets to avoid being locked into reliance on traditional energy solutions that result in local and global environmental and public health damage and carry the risk of assets being stranded. It also recognizes the importance of mainstreaming the new energy policy across the goals and policies that ADB supports more widely.

The policy emphasizes the still-unmet goal of universal access to energy; recognizes climate risks, costs, and mitigation opportunities; and proposes a course of action to respond to the scale and urgency of climate change management. In developing the new policy, ADB also considered the common but differentiated responsibilities of its DMCs and their commitments under the Sustainable Development Agenda and the Paris Agreement, and aims to ensure that the energy transition to low-carbon sources is realistic, flexible, and just.

The policy is consistent with Strategy 2030 and its seven operational priorities, since it aligns sovereign and nonsovereign energy operations with ADB's vision of a prosperous, inclusive, resilient, and sustainable Asia and the Pacific. The policy is also aligned with the Paris Agreement's imperative to make finance flows consistent with a pathway toward low GHG emissions and climate-resilient development. ADB will help DMCs to update and strengthen their NDCs and long-term strategies for decarbonization. ADB will align its financing with the mitigation and adaptation goals of the Paris Agreement, for 100% of sovereign operations and 85% of nonsovereign operations by July 2023, and 100% of nonsovereign operations by July 2025. ADB will provide staff guidance on this commitment and the operational methodologies to meet it, and ensure that the policy and its implementation will be congruent with not just climate change policy but also gender policy, safeguards policy, the fragile and conflict-affected situations and small island developing states approach, knowledge management action plans, principles for quality infrastructure investment, and others.

To achieve these objectives, ADB's energy sector operations will be based on the following policy principles:

(i)   **Policy principle 1:** ADB will support efforts to bring affordable, reliable, sustainable, and modern energy to all, so as to eradicate extreme poverty and reduce social inequalities.

(ii)   **Policy principle 2:** ADB will provide support to its DMCs to tackle climate change, enhance environmental sustainability, and build climate and disaster resilience.

(iii) **Policy principle 3:** ADB will support the institutional development, financial sustainability, and good governance of energy sector institutions and companies, as well as private sector participation. It will also help create the policy frameworks needed to manage the energy transition.

(iv)   **Policy principle 4:** ADB will promote regional energy cooperation and the integration of energy systems to strengthen energy security and increase cross-border access to cleaner energy sources.

(v)   **Policy principle 5:** ADB will continue to combine finance, knowledge, partnerships, and its country-focused approach to deliver integrated solutions with comprehensive and magnified development impacts.

The link between these guiding principles and the operational priorities 1–7 (OP1–OP7) of Strategy 2030 is shown in Appendix 2. The principles will be operationalized as follows:

A.   Principle 1: Securing Energy for a Prosperous and Inclusive Asia and the Pacific

The first policy principle obligates ADB to work toward securing energy for a prosperous and inclusive Asia and the Pacific by promoting distribution networks that increase access to power, light, clean cooking and drinking water, and clean heating and cooling. This principle is aligned with the objective of OP1 to address remaining poverty and reduce inequalities. Ensuring access to modern forms of energy improves well-being and creates opportunities for productive activities, including employment and businesses for those living in rural settings and informal settlements. Modern energy access also contributes to reducing persistent gender gaps, gender inequality, and women's burden of care and unpaid work, as called for in OP2. ADB will promote energy access through various approaches, including those described in the following paragraphs, and electric mobility will help make cities more livable by improving ambient air quality, as called for in OP4. Renewable energy development contributes to rural development, particularly through off-grid electrification programs and through wider access to clean energy as per SDG7, and contributes to food security in rural communities, as called for in OP5. ADB will help DMCs to secure energy for development by supporting electrification programs; promoting cleaner cooking, heating, and cooling; improving energy efficiency across supply and consumption chains; and promoting social inclusion, gender equality, and partnerships.

Eastern Indonesia Renewable Energy Project (Phase 2). Nurul Hidayah and Fatma Mulyana, staff of Vena Energy Solar Farm, are doing operation and maintenance work at Selong in Lombok Island.

Supporting Electrification Programs

ADB will focus intently on supporting DMCs with their electrification programs. People without access to modern energy are often not only energy-constrained but—compared with the rest of the population—may also have inferior social services and infrastructure for water, sanitation, transport, health, and education. Strategy 2030 clearly emphasizes tackling remaining poverty and reducing inequalities as well as promoting social inclusiveness. Achieving universal access can address many of these issues. ADB will support the extension of existing grids where appropriate and the deployment of new technologies such as renewable-energy-based microgrids and home systems, and also encourage the participation of local communities, to achieve full electrification.

Promoting Cleaner Cooking, Heating, and Cooling

ADB will promote cleaner cooking and heating solutions across DMCs. It will pursue the replacement of inefficient biomass cooking stoves with clean modern cooking stoves using alternative fuels such as liquefied petroleum gas and pellet gasification. ADB is also aware that it is important to consider electricity for cooking when analyzing and designing rural and urban electrification projects, while recognizing that this has implications for the system design. In promoting cleaner cooking, ADB will engage directly with women and other end users in terms of needs, technology acceptance, and financial sustainability.

ADB will support the construction, expansion, efficiency improvement, and rehabilitation of district heating networks. District heating through centralized heat production—often in combined heat and power plants or by using waste heat, heat pumps, geothermal, and natural gas—and through district or citywide insulated distribution networks is more efficient and cleaner than decentralized heating in buildings through smaller boilers. District heating for densely populated areas delivers higher energy efficiency, lower airborne pollution levels, and more comfortable living conditions. ADB will maximize the economies of scope and scale of district heating systems, apply advanced technologies, and establish the appropriate policy environment to realize multiple co-benefits from district heating projects. Heating infrastructure is essential in most Central and East Asian DMCs.

ADB will promote clean and efficient heating supply solutions. Electricity and renewable energy were introduced to heating to replace fossil fuels. Heat pump technology is the key driver in the transition because it is powered by electricity, the production of which is gradually being decarbonized. Heat pumps can draw heat from a wide variety of sources, which is one of the technology's major competitive advantages. The most frequently used energy sources include outdoor air, building exhaust air, shallow-ground geothermal, vertical heat wells, river water, sea water, city sewage water, industrial exhaust heat sources, and medium-deep geothermal energy. ADB will work with DMCs to ensure that they can benefit from using heat pump technology. This involves knowledge generation and demonstration projects that help leverage project financing.

ADB will promote clean and efficient cooling solutions. Growing economic prosperity and global warming mean that the demand for temperature-controlled buildings and for cold chain logistics in product delivery is accelerating in Asia and the Pacific. Air conditioners and electric fans represent one-fifth of the global electricity consumption in buildings. An escalating increase in the use of air conditioners puts electricity generation and distribution infrastructure under stress and contributes to higher GHG emissions. ADB will support DMCs in devising the necessary policies and investment programs to introduce modern technology, such as energy-efficient air-conditioning and the use of renewable energy for cooling solutions. At the same time, energy efficiency measures for cooling should not lead to greater use of fluorocarbons, including hydrofluorocarbons, which contribute to higher GHG emissions. ADB will support DMCs in gradually minimizing hydrofluorocarbons as scheduled by the Kigali Amendment to the Montreal Protocol, and will coordinate these efforts with efficient cooling support to adequately address life-cycle fluorocarbon management.[20] The cooling capacity of absorption chillers, which are driven almost entirely by heat, does not contribute to peak electricity demand. Therefore, many new solutions introduced for district heating are also applicable to the cooling of large buildings, or are driving district cooling systems for shopping malls, educational institutions, hospitals, hotels, and residential complexes. These systems also use waste heat from industrial processes, solar collectors, and geothermal heat.

Improving Energy Efficiency across Supply and Consumption Chains

ADB will support demand-side energy efficiency planning. Energy efficiency targets and plans should be carefully designed to meet the needs of individual DMCs in line with their implementation capabilities. Such plans can also draw on examples and best policy practices that countries within and outside the Asia and Pacific region have successfully used to ensure energy efficiency. ADB will promote minimum energy performance standards for appliances and equipment, fuel economy standards for vehicles, standards

---

[20] ADB is a signatory of the Initiative on Fluorocarbons Life Cycle Management. The life-cycle management of fluorocarbons requires the (i) development, manufacture, and use of refrigerants with zero or low global warming potential as an alternative to fluorocarbons, including replacement of old cooling equipment (upstream); and (ii) recovery, recycling, and destruction of the discarded fluorocarbons (midstream and downstream).

for electric motors in industry, mandatory energy audits and energy management policies for large industrial and commercial companies, and building codes. Codes, standards, and obligations, however, are not effective without properly planned enforcement mechanisms. The standards and measures that ADB will promote have already proven effective under local circumstances and in consumer behavior. They will take into consideration affordability for the targeted consumer group, given the trade-offs between the higher first costs of more efficient buildings, vehicles, and appliances versus the benefits that accrue later through better energy efficiency.

ADB will promote increased demand-side energy efficiency through policy support, use of innovative financing instruments, and mobilization of private sector resources. It will provide DMCs with technical assistance, grants, and loans to establish legal and regulatory frameworks, policies, and programs that support energy efficiency; and develop incentive mechanisms for consumers, utilities, energy service companies, and other market players. ADB will also assist DMCs in removing downstream and upstream barriers to energy efficiency based on their national circumstances. It will boost energy efficiency in its DMCs by collaborating with industry associations, banks, and specialized energy efficiency agencies, including providing loans for onlending under the financial intermediary loan modality. This will channel programs through locally based entities. ADB may combine financing with capacity building and technical assistance to help consolidate scattered industrial, commercial, and residential opportunities and induce behavioral changes for energy conservation.

ADB will promote increased efficiency in transmission and distribution networks. T&D losses and inefficiencies remain a significant problem in many DMCs. ADB will keep supporting their efforts to increase supply-side energy efficiency by building on its experience in reducing losses in electricity T&D. This includes using the latest technologies, such as high-temperature, low-sag conductors that can withstand higher operating temperatures and carry more power than conventional conductors, and dynamic line rating to help maximize load. ADB also supports the use of drones with advanced sensors for inspection and maintenance of transmission lines to identify and mitigate any risks to the power distribution network and enhance the safety of maintenance staff. Moreover, ADB will support the use of digital technologies such as smart meters to support demand-side energy efficiency.

Promoting Social Inclusion, Gender Equality, and Partnerships

ADB will promote inclusiveness in energy access activities. The preparation and implementation of ADB activities will factor in the needs of women, poor people, racial and ethnic minorities, indigenous peoples, people with disabilities, older persons, and other marginalized people. The responsibilities for electrification should be allocated to those sector entities with the necessary human, technical, and financial resources for the task, as well as the incentive to bring the process determinedly forward. Energy access planning will also consider community needs for safety and social development, such as street lighting, health centers, and schools, and the appropriate business model to ensure their sustainable use. ADB will involve communities in planning the operation, maintenance, and commercial services of systems when executing its energy access projects. Off-grid systems also create new localized employment and business opportunities in sales, installation, and maintenance of the distributed grids, and of end-use equipment. ADB will support related skills development and training in local communities.

ADB will promote gender equality in its energy operations. In promoting gender equality in its sector projects, ADB will enable women to take advantage of emerging opportunities in the energy transition and work to dismantle the structural barriers that have hindered women's participation in the sector. In line with OP2 objectives, it will help its DMCs reduce still-prevailing gender inequalities in energy access, and will include gender designs that are informed by women's different energy needs and gender roles. Women will be consulted and meaningfully included, gender analysis will be conducted, and sex-disaggregated data will be collected to inform project designs and ensure that gender is mainstreamed throughout the project cycle. ADB recognizes that women are not only beneficiaries or stakeholders but also key agents of change in energy transition. It will therefore promote and support women's participation in energy policy- and decision-making, provide leadership training, and foster their participation in green jobs. Women's entrepreneurship offers an opportunity to expand energy access and address energy poverty by empowering them, so ADB will pay particular attention to women's involvement in the supply chain as energy entrepreneurs. This will include support for women to overcome institutional biases and barriers, including lack of access to finance, and to strengthen the capacity of their energy businesses. ADB will also work to promote gender balance in the energy sector, where women are an underutilized source of talent and have been historically excluded.

ADB will promote partnership and innovation to deliver access to energy services. ADB will champion the use of new business models and financing solutions to overcome economic constraints on electrification efforts wherever access is lagging. It will also promote private sector participation, including local community investments, in electrification programs. It will complement its own resources and expertise by partnering with other development partners and civil society organizations in the design and execution of energy access investment programs.

B.   Principle 2: Building a Sustainable and Resilient Energy Future

The second principle highlights the operational activities that respond to OP3 (tackling climate change, building climate and disaster resilience, and enhancing environmental sustainability). ADB will assist DMCs in managing these critical tasks by increasing energy efficiency and the use of renewable and low-carbon energy, as well as integrating climate and disaster resilience considerations into energy sector operations. ADB will withdraw from financing new coal-fired power and heating plants, support DMCs in achieving a planned phaseout of coal in the Asia and Pacific region, and foster a just transition that considers its impacts on people and communities. ADB's support for clean and sustainable energy solutions—such as supply and demand-side energy efficiency, renewable energy, distributed renewable energy generation, and electric mobility—will help make cities more livable by improving ambient air quality, as called for by OP4. ADB will also support associated infrastructure such as smart and resilient power grids and BESSs to ensure the integration of an increasing share of renewable energy sources. In supporting energy

Cyclone Gita Recovery Project in Tonga. The project reconstructed and climate- and disaster-proofed the Nuku'alofa electricity network damaged by the cyclone in February 2018.

infrastructure investments, ADB considers the need to maintain biodiversity and healthy ecosystems by respecting environmental safeguards.

ADB will facilitate the transition to sustainable, lower-carbon, and resilient energy systems by assisting DMCs in:

(i)   accelerating the deployment of renewable energy,
(ii)   pursuing strategic decarbonization and the phaseout of coal,
(iii)   increasing the climate resilience of energy infrastructure, and
(iv)   ensuring a just transition.

Accelerating Renewable Energy

ADB will support the transition to cleaner power systems by helping accelerate the deployment of renewable energy. Recognizing that long-term decarbonization targets require a wide portfolio of technologies, ADB will champion the deployment of sustainable hydropower,[21] solar PV installations and concentrated solar facilities for electricity, solar energy from collectors for heating, onshore and offshore wind power, floating solar PV systems, sustainably sourced bioenergy, and geothermal energy. It will also assist DMCs in accessing next-generation renewable energy technologies, such as those that harness tidal and wave energy. As part of this effort, ADB will help develop an enabling environment through appropriate policies, sector reforms, and capacity building.

---

[21]   International Hydropower Association. 2021. Hydropower Sustainability Tools (accessed 2 July 2021).

ADB will be selective in its support for storage hydropower plants, including pumped-storage hydro plants. Small hydro plants, such as run-of-river plants, will be subject to standard technical and safeguard assessments. ADB will support large hydropower schemes that have been evaluated in a robust environmental and social assessment, including an ecologically led e-flow assessment, and after consideration of alternative locations and designs.[22] For all hydro plants, particular attention will be paid to ensuring an eco-sensitive design, compensation for land acquisition and resettlement, and livelihood restoration in accordance with ADB's safeguard policy as well as international good practice for large hydropower projects. In view of the number of aging hydropower plants in the Asia and Pacific region and the associated risks, ADB will assist DMCs in rehabilitating or replacing structures as well as electrical, mechanical, and electromechanical equipment.

ADB will support the deployment of various kinds of energy storage to enhance system flexibility for greater renewable energy contributions. Thanks to declining costs, storage technologies, especially BESS, can now be more readily deployed, and their use can smooth the load curve of renewable energy generation, provide peaking and reserve capacity, and help maintain frequency in the grid. BESS may also serve as a viable alternative to diesel-powered generation units for backup services. Household batteries, too, can contribute to managing peak demand, improving the load factor, and reducing network congestion. Since the deployment of BESS will lead to a buildup of used batteries, which may be classified as hazardous waste depending on the battery technology, ADB will also help DMCs establish regulations to properly recycle or dispose of them in accordance with international best practices.

ADB will support waste-to-energy investments for heat or electricity, provided that the feedstock for combustion results from a prudent order of waste management priorities.[23] Waste-to-energy investments can improve local environments and health in cities and rural areas by removing the environmental hazards caused by open waste dumping and open burning. ADB will support projects that promote a circular economy and consider holistically the order of priorities—first reducing waste generation, then exploiting the options for reusing and recycling materials, then using waste to recover energy or usable materials, followed by sanitary engineered landfilling as the last option. ADB support for waste-to-energy investments will promote sustainable livelihood opportunities for the poorest people working along the waste value chain and at landfills. The potential environmental and social impacts of waste-to-energy investments will be managed by using the best internationally available technologies in the design and operation of such projects in accordance with international conventions.

ADB will consider biodiversity and other environmental impacts in its support for renewable energy planning and deployment. The low-carbon transition will increase the volume of solar and wind energy in use, ensuring close alignment with key objectives under OP3. It will also require expanded electricity T&D networks and set new requirements for mitigating projects' environmental and biodiversity impacts and sensitivities, which differ from those of past fuel-based or hydropower projects. Solar, wind, and transmission projects, for example, have little effect on inland waters, but they cover more expansive

---

[22]   International Commission on Large Dams. 2021. Definition of a Large Dam (accessed 15 July 2021).
[23]   ADB. 2020. *Waste to Energy in the Age of the Circular Economy: Best Practice Handbook.* Manila.

areas of land and sea and have an impact on birdlife. Risks should be avoided or mitigated through effective early planning and use of appropriate technological solutions.

Role of Specific Energy Sources in Pursuing Strategic Decarbonization

ADB will support the decarbonization of industrial processes. Industry accounts for the largest share in total final consumption in the Asia and Pacific region. Many industrial processes are difficult to decarbonize, including those requiring very high temperatures that cannot be met by high-efficiency heat pumps or solar thermal systems, and those requiring fuel to contribute to a chemical process. ADB will explore solutions that include interventions beyond the power generation subsector to decarbonize the various direct uses of fossil fuels through electricity-based processes, such as direct electric heating, electric arc and induction heating, and green and blue hydrogen. Through knowledge sharing and demonstration projects, ADB will bring emerging solutions to benefit the region's industrial growth.

ADB will support limited downstream oil projects where necessary, but will not support upstream or midstream oil projects. It may support projects with electricity solutions involving petroleum-based systems along with renewable energy for isolated grids, remote areas, and in fragile and conflict-affected situations—if configurations without fossil-fuel components are technically, economically, and financially not viable and if there is a clear plan to reduce the energy system's dependence on fossil fuel by enhancing renewable energy and/or renewable energy storage solutions over time. ADB may continue providing guarantees and loans to partner banks in DMCs that support international trade and supply chains, which may involve trading in oil to support the immediate flows required to keep economies running in a few countries where there is little private sector support for such import risk. This support may be extended until coordination between multilateral development banks produces a shared approach to trade and supply chain financing in line with the Paris Agreement. ADB will not finance any oil exploration, drilling, or extraction activities.

ADB will not support coal mining, processing, storage, and transportation, nor any new coal-fired power generation. Since coal is a main source of GHGs and air pollution in the Asia and Pacific region, new coal-fired capacity is not compatible with the long-term environmental plans of DMCs. ADB confirms its current practice of not financing new coal-based capacity for power and heat. ADB will promote the adoption of cleaner fuel sources and will support emissions reductions that mitigate health and environmental impacts but will not participate in investments to modernize, upgrade, or renovate coal facilities that will extend the life of existing coal-fired power and heating capacity. ADB will support the early retirement of coal-based power plants and the enhancement of power generation dispatch regimes to discourage the use of high-emitting, inefficient coal-fired power plants. It will also assist the decommissioning of coal-fired power plants and site redevelopment for new economic activity, including the removal and secure management of hazardous materials, restoration of soil and water quality, redevelopment of buildings, and upgrades of existing infrastructure. In providing support for the phasing-out of coal, ADB will also help create new jobs in cooperation with the local communities and stakeholders. Comprehensive planning for a just transition will underpin these operations.

ADB will not support any natural gas exploration or drilling activities, and will be selective in its support for midstream and downstream natural gas. ADB recognizes that natural gas has a role to play as a transitional fuel that can support power system flexibility under specific circumstances. ADB may also support projects that improve universal access to modern and clean energy for electricity and cooking for those without access. Natural gas investments may also be supported if they serve space heating, cooling, domestic demand, industrial energy applications, or distributed electricity generation to improve energy access, provided it is demonstrated that the projects displace more polluting fuels. ADB may finance investments in natural gas infrastructure—including gas T&D pipelines, LNG terminals, and storage facilities—and natural gas-based end-use facilities subject to a set of screening criteria consistent with the Paris Agreement. ADB's support for natural gas-based power generation will be conditional on evidence that the project employs high-efficiency and internationally best available technologies, reduces emissions by directly displacing other fossil-fuel-based thermal power capacity, or results in a lower grid emission factor estimated as an average over its operational life. In addition, all projects involving natural gas must meet all of the following conditions:

(i)   No other low-carbon or zero-carbon technology, or combination thereof, can provide the same service at an equivalent or lower cost at a comparable scale.[24]

(ii) The project's operating lifetime is consistent with the carbon stabilization trajectory aiming to achieve carbon neutrality by about 2050, and by a time set by DMCs that is consistent with their NDCs. The project also avoids long-term lock-in into carbon infrastructure and the associated risk of creating stranded assets.

(iii) The project is economically viable considering the social cost of carbon and an operating lifetime consistent with condition (ii).

ADB will support carbon capture, use, and storage technologies for power plants, liquefied natural gas import facilities, and industries. ADB will continue to provide capacity development, technical assistance, finance, and regulatory advice in support of DMC programs to identify and remove hurdles to the development, demonstration, and commercialization of CCUS systems. The aim is to enable energy transition initiatives, including the development of applications such as blue hydrogen with net GHG reductions. ADB recognizes the crucial role of these technologies in the long term, particularly for industrial activities that are difficult to decarbonize, and will help DMCs to plan, finance, and deploy such systems. ADB will not finance CCUS in the context of enhanced oil recovery.

ADB will support the use of advanced biofuels in DMCs to reduce their dependence on oil and their transport sector emissions. Liquid and gaseous fuels represent another important avenue for providing a stable energy supply and storing energy from various renewable sources, including sustainably sourced biomass, waste, and variable renewable electricity. In the future, sustainable and ecologically friendly biofuels, and synthetic fuels based on sustainable green and blue hydrogen and carbon capture, may also provide

---

[24]   "Same service" means that the proposed supply option must provide the same quantity of energy requirements at all times, including the ability to supply demand variations, at the same quality of voltage and frequency, and with the same reliability with respect to interruptions.

alternatives that can replace the use of fossil fuels in various industries, while at the same time not undermining food security. To that end, ADB will support DMCs in developing and using advanced biofuels; this includes helping them build larger, centralized biogas units that produce methane for power generation, transport, or for sale to the natural gas network.

ADB will not finance investments in nuclear energy. ADB recognizes the role of nuclear energy in the low-carbon transition given its ability to provide low-carbon baseload electricity, and will include nuclear analysis in the development of long-term energy plans and climate strategies, as appropriate. However, ADB will not finance investments in nuclear power given the many barriers to its deployment, including risks related to nuclear proliferation, waste management and safety issues, and very high investment costs relative to ADB's resources.

Increasing the Resilience and Efficiency of Electricity Infrastructure

ADB will support DMCs in building higher resilience in the transmission and distribution subsector. Managing climate change and disaster risks requires ensuring the resilience of all electricity infrastructure, including T&D systems, and considering the risks from climate change, natural hazards, malicious attacks, and human errors. ADB will assist DMCs in improving the reliability of electricity supply, connecting additional supply capacity to the grid, reducing technical losses and power theft, and reaching outlying and previously unserved regions. ADB will help deploy digital technologies such as smart meters to reduce technical and commercial losses and encourage demand-side energy efficiency, peer-to-peer trading using blockchain technology for energy markets, and artificial intelligence for predictive grid management and grid resilience. ADB may also support the use of advanced conductors, dynamic line rating, advanced grid control systems such as anti-blackout technology, various demand-response mechanisms, on-grid electricity storage, distributed generation, cybersecurity, and digital smart grid solutions, which are among the available options to increase grid reliability, flexibility, and resilience.

ADB will support energy utilities in addressing their environmental liabilities. Transformers in some DMCs may still contain polychlorinated biphenyls and need to be removed from service, or dechlorinated by 2025 and disposed of by 2028 under the Stockholm Convention. ADB will support these efforts. In addition, ADB will help DMCs set up emission control and battery disposal standards, and encourage the use of alternatives to sulfur hexafluoride—the most potent GHG—in gas-insulated switchgear substations. Furthermore, ADB will pursue opportunities to maintain the contiguity and integrity of the ecosystems impacted by electricity T&D infrastructure, beyond mitigating negative environmental impacts as acceptable costs.

Ensuring a Just Transition

ADB will support DMCs in undertaking and implementing transparent and inclusive planning and policies for a just transition. The transition to a carbon-neutral economy will affect every aspect of how we produce goods and provide services, particularly in conventional energy industries. It will considerably affect workers and communities, as well as future jobs and demand for skills. Planning for a just transition will be critical in managing this process: the aim is to mitigate negative socioeconomic impacts and increase opportunities associated with the transition; support affected workers and communities; and enhance access to sustainable, inclusive, and resilient livelihoods for all. ADB will work with DMCs to support such planning in a way that involves all stakeholders and affected groups at all stages of the energy transition.

C.   Principle 3: Supporting Institutions, Private Sector Participation, and Good Governance

The third principle contributes to OP6 by strengthening governance and institutional capacity. Universal access, climate goals, and technological innovations are accelerating change in power generation. ADB will support associated energy sector reforms, such as strengthening regulatory frameworks and introducing competitive markets and market-based instruments, including carbon pricing. Strengthening DMCs' institutions will allow them to manage the sector efficiently, introduce progressive and enabling energy policies, attract private sector investment, and achieve the long-term financial sustainability of energy entities by ensuring the financial viability of investments and the maintenance of infrastructure assets. This principle also recognizes that good governance includes environmental and social considerations, so energy generation, transmission, and distribution companies should adopt corporate policies and procedures on pollution control and waste management, health and safety, and gender equality. Throughout this work, ADB will continue to operate consistently with the G20 Principles for Quality Infrastructure Investment, emphasizing the importance of integrating economic efficiency,

Sermsang Khushig Khundii Solar Project in Mongolia. The project involves the construction, operation, and maintenance of a 15-megawatt solar plant in Khushig valley, Tuv *aimag*.

environmental and social considerations, climate resilience, and stricter governance in all operations.

Supporting Institutions

ADB will help DMCs in strengthening the quality and capacity of energy sector institutions to undertake policy reforms. Whether focusing on expanding electrification, energy efficiency, or the integration of more renewable energy into the grid, the desired outcomes of policies and plans can only be achieved if government institutions, sector utilities, and companies in DMCs are financially sound and operationally efficient, and have skilled and capable employees. ADB's energy sector reform activities will be carefully tailored and sequenced to achieve the desired policy outcomes, taking into consideration the political and economic context of each DMC. The reforms will target good governance and efficiency of operations, the ability to attract and implement investments, and financial independence and sustainability of sector utilities and companies. The reforms should lead to measurable improvements in the security, quality, affordability, resilience, and environmental sustainability of energy supply.

ADB will support institutions in adopting stronger environmental and social policies. It will encourage energy sector institutions, utilities, and companies in DMCs to increase diversity and improve the gender balance in their workforce by providing equal opportunities for women and to remove barriers to their inclusion and career advancement. ADB will also assist these institutions, utilities, and companies in increasing their corporate sustainability by introducing or reinforcing internal pollution control and waste policies and procedures, ensuring compliance with national laws and regulations, and strengthening internal labor and health and safety policies and procedures.

ADB will help increase the operational efficiencies and commercialization of loss-making distribution utilities. Electricity distribution utilities and companies are the primary contact point for end users of electricity, including consumers in low-income and vulnerable groups; and many of the deficiencies in service quality must be rectified at the distribution level. Power distribution also needs to be transformed and modernized to meet new demands for cooling, e-mobility, smart meters, and the Internet of Things to facilitate energy efficiency and the integration of distributed renewable energy sources. ADB will support distribution companies in achieving financial soundness and more efficient operations, which will be key to allowing for such modernization. ADB will also assist the introduction of performance-based regulations to motivate natural distribution monopolies to improve their operations.

Tariff and Subsidy Reform

ADB will support the adoption of equitable and cost-reflective tariff structures. It will advise on reforms designed to create sound electricity tariff structures and time-of-use pricing that reflect the full cost of the operations, promote energy efficiency, and penalize peak-hour and peak-season electricity consumption. It will also advise on approaches to protect vulnerable groups of consumers when removing electricity subsidies, such as the introduction of lifeline tariffs and smart meters. ADB will also support tariff structures that consider the needs of new consumers from vulnerable groups, particularly customers from poor and marginalized households, and households headed by women, for whom connection charges may be prohibitive. Support for these groups should be recognized by regulation and funded equitably.

ADB will encourage DMCs to phase out energy subsidies that create unwanted distortions. International experience shows that a comprehensive package of policies is necessary to ensure that reforms that phase out energy subsidies lead to the right incentives, and to an ultimately successful and sustainable policy change. A reform strategy ideally factors in pricing mechanisms and institutions, the impacts of the reforms, and the political economy barriers. ADB will support DMCs in developing such a strategy and ensuring that it includes welfare measures that shield poor and vulnerable people from high fuel prices, as well as independent pricing mechanisms, public awareness and support campaigns, and consultation and communication programs.

Private Sector Participation

ADB will catalyze private investments in sustainable energy projects in the region. It will continue to support PPPs and independent power producers as vehicles for attracting private capital into the energy sector. It will provide direct financing to companies, banks, financial intermediaries, and projects that increase clean energy and energy efficiency in the region. ADB will make available loans and equity, credit enhancements, and risk mitigation instruments, but also policy advice and support for the preparation and structuring of projects. It will provide transaction advisory services and assistance in drafting project agreements and managing the procurement processes. Through these activities, ADB will promote sustainability, integrity and transparency, high standards of corporate governance, gender equality, and social and environmental safeguards, and help manage market failures without distorting the market.

ADB will support increased competition and private sector participation in DMCs' energy markets. Private sector participation can lead to higher operational efficiency, cost-effectiveness, and better responsiveness to customer needs. Private actors are expected to contribute greater dynamism to the energy sector and be better able to take advantage of opportunities created by new technologies and business models. ADB will support the next generation of electricity market reforms, focused on open access to transmission systems and retail competition. It will offer assistance in the unbundling of vertically integrated utilities, the corporatization of specific utility functions, securitization, asset recycling, and—if requested—the privatization of public enterprises created in the process. ADB will also support strong regulatory agencies and carefully designed regulation to steer the operations of national T&D companies.

Greater Impact through Sector-Wide Long-Term Planning

ADB will support DMCs in preparing long-term energy strategies and policies that include the phaseout of coal in power generation. ADB will assist energy planning based on a systematic analysis of technology options, costs, and social and environmental impacts. Such analysis should include three key quantitative and time-bound targets: (i) decrease in CO_2 emission intensity, (ii) peaking of CO_2 emissions, and (iii) achievement of carbon neutrality. ADB will seek to support appropriate policy developments that would help DMCs achieve these targets, and will finance priority investments arising from those strategies.

ADB will support planning processes that consider both constraints and inputs from consultations. Decision-making relies increasingly on technical, social, environmental, and economic assessments to inform policy development and to set national targets. Planning and simulation should consider not only cost–benefit assessments but also constraints stemming from climate change, sustainability, resilience, and social equity demands. The planning process should be consultative—from the creation of various scenarios for planning, modeling, and testing, to the setting of criteria and indexes for a multicriteria analysis of the outcomes—and result in choosing the recommended way forward for the energy sector. ADB will also support an enabling institutional structure to deliver and implement such an integrated energy plan at a time when the energy sector is increasingly decentralized and deregulated.

ADB will prioritize financing for investments identified in a long-term planning process. Sector-wide, long-term plans inform the dialogue between DMCs and ADB on policy design and institutional reforms, infrastructure financing, and improvements to the electricity markets. Integrated resource plans, energy and power system master plans, and consequent road maps and subsector-specific plans also inform the dialogue between DMCs and ADB, and facilitate project due diligence while reducing project transaction costs and time. Such long-term plans should be supported by strategic environmental and social assessments. For example, a strategic environmental assessment of transmission or renewable energy master plans could help ensure that resulting projects are environmentally sustainable and that location constraints were considered upfront.

ADB will continue to assist DMCs in enhancing their climate ambitions. ADB will help refine energy strategies to align them with the goals set out in DMCs' NDCs and long-term climate strategies, and identify energy sector and cross-sector projects that can translate climate goals into action. ADB will work with DMCs on mobilizing the required skills, technology, and financing to implement their priority projects. It will provide a dedicated technical assistance platform to continue this work, help build capacity, and provide knowledge and other support needed to implement the NDCs. During the 2020s, DMCs will face two rounds of updating their NDCs, and ADB will assist them in this process.

ADB will incorporate resilience planning into its support for long-term energy planning. Long-term energy planning will consider the impacts of climate change, such as hydrological changes, accelerated growth of biomass with consequences for renewable energy production, and an increasing number of hot summertime days that stress the electricity system with high peak volumes and demand for cooling energy. ADB will support DMCs in integrating an assessment of these impacts and consequent investment considerations into their long-term energy supply strategies and national adaptation plans.

ADB will assist DMCs in updating and revising their electrification plans. ADB will help its DMCs develop a national master plan with coherent priority targets and implementation plans to achieve them, including for last-mile household connections. Planning can be supported by multicriteria techniques that apply geospatial least-cost algorithms via satellite imaging. A transparent, impartial, and socially sensitive multicriteria analysis is needed to guide the choice between national grid extension and off-grid solutions. It is also needed to identify the type of off-grid solution best suited for each population center, and to set the implementation schedule so that off-grid solutions can be made "grid ready" for future connection to the national grid. The most successful electrification strategies are based on a high-level political commitment to electrification, which ADB's sustained policy engagement with and continued capacity building of its DMCs can help ensure.

Partnering to Shape Energy Reform Policies

ADB will support the development of enabling policy frameworks for the provision of affordable, reliable, and sustainable energy; and to manage the transition to low-carbon energy. Well-designed enabling policy frameworks with programmatic interventions through well-sequenced programs, policies, and regulations serve as risk mitigation instruments for sustainable energy projects. The energy landscape is changing ever more quickly, and policies must be adjusted to integrate emerging new technologies and business models. They must also consider the specific circumstances of each DMC and maintain an appropriate degree of stability, future orientation, and transparency to ensure investor confidence. The range of possible enabling policy measures is extensive and includes technology-neutral policies such as carbon trading and tax, and highly specific regulation aimed at individual technologies, such as building codes for energy efficiency or feed-in tariffs for the accelerated deployment of certain renewable technologies. ADB will help DMCs to learn from international experience for their policy design, including successful and failed policy measures. Several examples confirm that seemingly small weaknesses in the details of regulations may cause policy measures to fail.

ADB will support greater use of carbon pricing instruments in the region. Carbon pricing is an integral part of the broader policy architecture and can be implemented in tandem with other policies, such as the removal of fossil-fuel subsidies. Clear and predictable carbon prices in domestic and international markets can encourage more efficient use of fossil fuels, reduce emissions, and enhance the economic viability of low-carbon technologies to help DMCs achieve the climate targets articulated under their respective NDCs cost-effectively. Carbon price signals can be achieved through carbon taxes, emission-trading systems, and international offset mechanisms. Carbon pricing can be effective in raising domestic revenues as well as mobilizing international carbon finance to encourage investments in advanced low-carbon technologies through international offset mechanisms. If designed and implemented appropriately, robust carbon pricing instruments can be effective in achieving an energy transition by accelerating the diffusion of advanced low-carbon technologies, enhancing the deployment of renewable energy technologies, accelerating e-mobility, encouraging fuel switching, and increasing the use of different forms of non-fossil-fuel energy.

ADB will continue to mobilize carbon finance to enable DMCs to participate in carbon markets. Carbon finance—mobilized through bilateral, regional, and international carbon markets—can lower financial barriers and facilitate cross-border trade of electricity, enhance the share of renewables in the overall electricity supply mix, and foster regional integration. Momentum is growing for the use of carbon pricing instruments in Asia and the Pacific, including domestic and bilateral as well as international carbon markets. ADB has a long-standing engagement with carbon markets, providing technical capacity building and mobilizing carbon finance to support GHG emission mitigation activities in the region. It will continue to adopt a holistic approach by mobilizing international carbon finance through its trust funds and providing technical support for policy development, capacity building, and the strengthening of institutional infrastructure to enhance the ability of DMCs to participate in and take advantage of emerging carbon markets.

ADB will support innovative clean technology deployment in its DMCs. ADB's technical assistance can help pilot technologies in DMCs that are crowdsourced through ADB's open innovation platform.[25] ADB also established the ADB Ventures Investment Fund to support impact technology startups and to leverage ADB's operational networks and industry expertise to generate technology-piloting opportunities in DMCs.

ADB will support policies and regulations that address emerging needs. ADB will help DMCs formulate the new types of policy measures and regulations that are needed as the reduced cost of wind and solar PV electricity increases the share of variable and intermittent electricity supply as well as distributed generation in electricity systems. The integration of renewable energies into existing systems calls for the reinforcement of ancillary services through energy storage, digitalization, and other innovative technologies, as well as grid management. Increased system flexibility is the property of the whole power system rather than its components. Creating flexibility therefore depends on a wide array of factors and requires the cooperative operation of assets by different independent entities in the power system, including power producers, district heating utilities, large consumers, grid owners and operators, market exchanges and single-buyer hosts, and government agencies. The challenge of regulation is to navigate this complex landscape to mobilize the flexibility resources effectively.

ADB will help DMCs plan and implement improved electricity market designs. Short-term efficiency can be achieved through competitive and optimized dispatch, while long-term efficiency requires sufficient price signals and incentives for investments in new resources to ensure adequate capacity. In supporting such market reforms, particular attention will be paid to the market design to ensure an optimal level of liquidity and to minimize opportunities for speculative market behavior that can cause large fluctuations and sharp spikes in prices. ADB will also support DMCs in building the institutional and technical capacities to operate the improved electricity markets.

D.   Principle 4: Promoting Regional Cooperation and Integration

The fourth principle—fostering regional cooperation and integration—is an operational priority of Strategy 2030 (OP7). ADB will promote regional cooperation through policy dialogue, knowledge sharing, and investments in electricity and natural gas network infrastructure and cross-border energy trading, such as building regional energy markets. The benefits of subregional and bilateral energy cooperation include cost savings, reduced

---

[25]   ADB. 2019. *Energy Sector Technology Innovation Challenge*. Manila.

South Asia Subregional Economic Cooperation Power System Expansion Project in Nepal. An aerial shot captures of the automated 220-kilovolt transmission substation—supported by ADB and built under the South Asia Subregional Economic Cooperation Power System Expansion Project—at Khurkot in Parbat.

GHG emissions and air pollution, and increased energy security by enabling more diverse energy mixes.

ADB will continue to support bilateral and subregional energy cooperation. Larger electricity balancing areas allow for higher shares of renewable energy in power systems, and the ideal balancing regions may even cross national borders. Transboundary trading of electricity and grid services can also improve energy security and system stability, and reduce generation costs and system losses. ADB will maximize subregional economic cooperation platforms such as the Greater Mekong Subregion Program, the Central Asia Regional Economic Cooperation, the South Asia Subregional Economic Cooperation Program, and the South Asian Association for Regional Cooperation, and has sustained its engagement with the Association of Southeast Asian Nations and countries in northeast Asia to promote regional cooperation. ADB's support for energy cooperation plays a significant role in all these contexts and has included power trade and natural gas pipeline projects. Its continued support will further advance these initiatives. ADB will also promote demand-side collaboration opportunities, such as harmonization of grid codes and other energy performance standards.

ADB will continue to support the expansion of cross-border energy trade and markets. ADB's assistance to DMCs on cross-border electricity trade has sought to overcome barriers and complexities in international and domestic politics and finance, as well as technical and operational risks. Moving from bilateral cross-border trade to subregional competitive markets has proven particularly challenging. However, ADB will continue to support knowledge sharing and intercountry dialogue to remove political barriers and strengthen cooperation. Overall, intensified transboundary economic cooperation contributes to maintaining and deepening peace and stability in the region.

ADB will support cross-border and subregional electricity development of interconnection infrastructure. To help DMCs meet their climate goals, ADB will prioritize projects that pursue the large-scale deployment of renewable energy resources and the integration of variable renewable electricity at scale to wide-area grids through electricity interconnections. It will refrain from supporting dedicated cross-border transmission lines where power generation is linked to coal-fired power plants. ADB will continue to encourage subregional interconnectivity initiatives in Central Asia, Southeast Asia, and South Asia while also exploring emerging possibilities for extended interconnectivity in other areas within the region.

E.   Principle 5: Integrated Cross-Sector Operations to Maximize Development Impact

The principle of integrated solutions responds to Strategy 2030's aim for ADB to be stronger, better, and faster in its delivery and to maximize the development impacts of cross-sector operations. ADB will integrate its energy expertise across sectors and themes to address more complex development challenges. It will continue to combine finance, knowledge, and partnerships in its energy operations. Its country-focused approach will deliver integrated energy and cross-sector solutions that provide comprehensive and magnified development impacts.

Access to Clean Energy Investment Program in Pakistan. Rooftop solar panels installed at a public elementary school in Punjab provide clean and reliable energy.

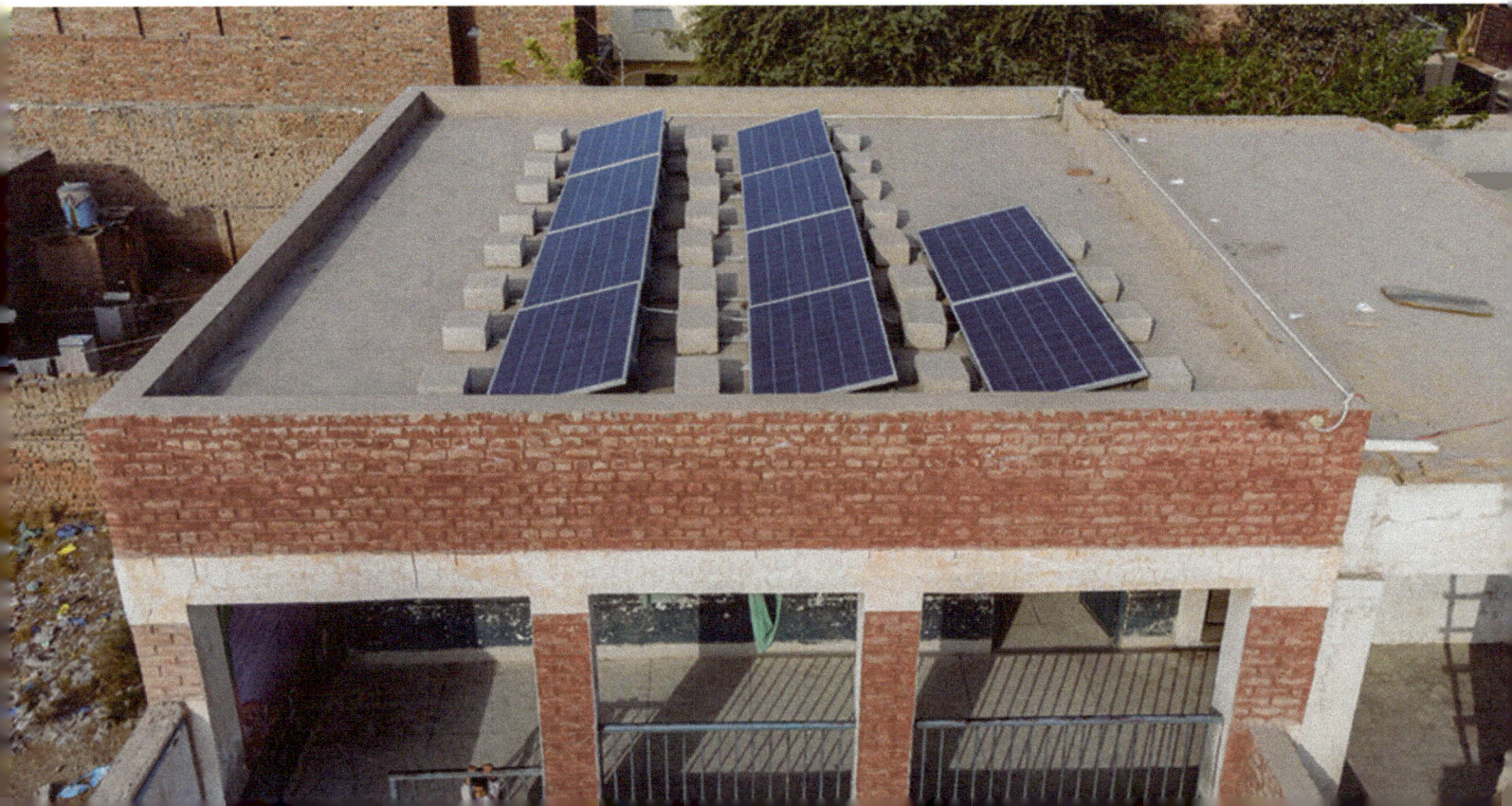

ADB will continue to use a wide range of financial instruments to support DMCs' energy needs. It will keep financing energy infrastructure and other interventions and provide associated technical assistance. Other instruments offer additional value for achieving the energy sector reforms still on the agenda of many of the region's DMCs. Policy-based lending is a long-standing modality to support reform agendas and has been increasingly used by some DMCs to support energy sector reforms, commercialization, and the enactment of new energy policies necessitated by more stringent climate commitments. Results-based lending and financial intermediation lending can be appropriate modalities for investment programs that increase energy access, reduce emissions, or increase the share of renewable energy. Sector loans are another modality that has proven to be effective. Private sector operations will continue to strengthen resource mobilization and cofinancing, supported by guarantees, syndications, risk transfers, and concessional financing for blended finance.

ADB will use financial intermediation as an approach to supporting dispersed subprojects. Financial intermediary loans can be used for expanding electrification, clean cooking, island energy supply, demand-side energy efficiency programs, and other programs that are not amenable to project loans or other investment modalities. ADB will apply the financial intermediary loan modality by partnering with national banks and specialized financial institutions.

ADB will support DMCs in developing their domestic markets for clean energy financing. Effective financing of clean energy projects is held back in some DMCs by their underdeveloped domestic financial systems and markets, which limit access to affordable local currency financing for investors in energy efficiency and clean energy. International finance can come in to fill certain gaps, but this in turn may expose investors to foreign exchange risk. A long-term sustainable solution would be to develop the depth and liquidity of domestic finance sectors, with the aim of creating a balanced mix of domestic and international finance flows to pursue energy efficiency and low-carbon energy. ADB is committed to helping DMCs develop their domestic capital markets by issuing local currency bonds and through other financial products, sound structuring and pricing of both sovereign and nonsovereign projects, and policy dialogue.

ADB will invest in and raise climate finance such as green bonds and other sustainability-linked debt and equity instruments for governments and the private sector. ADB can co-invest in green bond funds and provide credit enhancement to new issuances to realize clean energy investments in the region. Its management of risk exposures, particularly through guarantees, will help involve institutional and financial institutions with a longer-term horizon—such as pension funds and insurers—in sustainable energy projects. ADB will also seek to work with impact investors that are interested in developing green portfolios in the Asia and Pacific region.

ADB will partner with other development and energy institutions. Building on its strong track record of collaboration, ADB will continue to coordinate with multiple partners in the energy sector—other multilateral development banks, international development agencies, multilateral and bilateral institutions, private sector entities, academia, think tanks and research institutions, civil society organizations, community-based organizations, and philanthropic foundations—in formulating policies and designing, implementing, and monitoring projects. With the support of development partners, ADB established the Clean

Energy Financing Partnership Facility to facilitate the deployment of new, more efficient clean energy technologies, and assist policy, regulatory, and institutional reforms that encourage clean energy development.

ADB will leverage its experience to gather and share knowledge gained from energy operations. Through its activities with DMCs, ADB has accumulated a wealth of experience and knowledge on energy sector policies, structural and institutional setups, project designs and implementation, financial modalities, energy technologies and innovation, and on how all of these have fared in practice. ADB's interventions are subject to professional validation and evaluation against robust criteria for their relevance, effectiveness, efficiency, sustainability, and success. ADB will continue improving its processes to generate, capture, and disseminate knowledge, while also paying attention to collecting and documenting the valuable tacit knowledge accrued through its work. Knowledge will be shared internally so that staff can integrate it into day-to-day work. ADB also uses knowledge to support its DMCs by producing research, knowledge products, manuals, and advisory services that convey the best practices and lessons to shape DMCs' policies and regulations and to identify, assess, and implement programs and projects for their energy sector development and energy transition. ADB's energy operations also enable it to collect empirical evidence from DMCs on the performance of its green financing instruments. Through these data ADB can contribute, together with other multilateral development banks and key stakeholders, to refining the criteria, benchmarks, standards, and thematic focuses of climate and green financing mechanisms.

ADB will intensify partnerships for greater knowledge-sharing impacts. It will expand and nurture its knowledge partnerships with bilateral and multilateral agencies and institutions, think tanks, academia, civil society organizations, and the private sector. It will also continue its dialogues on critical energy sector issues with DMCs, development partners, the private sector, and civil societies within the framework of the Asia Clean Energy Forum. It will promote knowledge sharing across the institution and communicate externally through capacity building and advisory services, publications, training, and workshops. ADB will leverage diverse expertise and knowledge in a range of areas from across the institution, including from sovereign and nonsovereign collaboration, to develop integrated solutions with advanced technologies.

ADB will work across sector boundaries to help integrate modern energy access and support into a sustainable and just energy transition. Maximizing ADB's development impact in a rapidly changing and interconnected energy sector will require new and more comprehensive approaches. In accordance with the Paris Agreement, ADB will help DMCs work toward a just transition that addresses the dislocation and adjustment costs and takes into account the creation of decent work and quality jobs consistent with national development priorities. In its energy operations, ADB increasingly encounters proposals with development objectives in thematic areas outside energy, but with a considerable need for energy sector contributions. Conversely, the energy transition may cause, for example, the need for interventions by other sectors to support training and the re-skilling of energy sector workers as production methods and technology evolve to cleaner modes. ADB will provide DMCs with its knowledge and expertise through cross-sector and cross-thematic teams. This will enable DMCs to design new policies and manage demanding projects with broad and complex environmental, social, and economic implications.

VI. Implementation Arrangements

The policy applies to both ADB's sovereign and nonsovereign operations, including project loans, sector loans, policy-based loans, results-based loans, financial intermediary loans, guarantees, equity participation, and technical assistance. ADB's Energy Sector Group will prepare staff guidance elaborating upon the screening criteria for ADB operations involving natural gas, large hydropower plants, and waste-to-energy plants. The staff guidance notes will be updated, as needed, to reflect the criteria set forth in the joint methodology developed by the Multilateral Development Bank Working Group on Paris Alignment, in ADB's updated safeguard policy, and any other relevant policy or staff guidance issued after the approval of the 2021 Energy Policy.

The implementation of the energy policy will require adequate human and financial resources. The skills mix and technical capacity of ADB staff must be enhanced to deal with energy policy reforms, energy efficiency, and emerging low-carbon technologies. These human and financial resource requirements will be met by reprioritizing available staff and consultant positions under internal administrative budget funds, the Clean Energy Financing Partnership Facility, technical assistance, and other appropriate funding sources.

A review of the 2021 Energy Policy will be conducted in 2025 to assess the progress on the objectives of this policy to accelerate the development of sustainable and resilient energy systems that provide reliable and affordable access to all, foster inclusive economic growth and social development, and support the low-carbon transition in Asia and the Pacific. Human and financial resources will also be reviewed in 2025 to take stock of ADB's development effectiveness and ability to meet the requirements of DMCs in their long-term energy transition.

Floating Solar Energy Project in Viet Nam. ADB supported the installation of the first large-scale floating photovoltaic solar power facility in the country—also the largest in Southeast Asia.

Appendix

Table A1: Key Energy Guidance Publications of Multilateral Development Banks

Energy Policy Key Publications	Policy/ Strategy/ Other	Year of Launch	Highlights and Position on Fossil Fuels
AfDB Energy Policy 2012	P	2012	New Deal based on five principles: • Raising aspirations to solve Africa's energy challenges • Establishing a Transformative Partnership on Energy for Africa • Mobilizing domestic and international capital for innovative financing in Africa's energy sector • Supporting African governments in strengthening energy policy, regulation, and sector governance

New Energy Deal for Africa 2016	S	2016	• Increasing the African Development Bank's investments in energy and climate financing
			   – 2012 policy does not exclude coal, oil, and gas-fired power
			   – Oil and gas exploration activities will not be supported

ADB
 	
Energy Policy 2009
	P	2009	Three pillars:
			• Developing clean energy (energy efficiency, renewable energy, fuel switching)
			• Increasing energy access
			• Improving sector governance (necessary to bring in commercial investment).
			   – Coal-fired power in exceptional cases only.
			   – Coal mine and oil field development in exceptional cases only.
			   – Any oil and gas field exploration will not be financed.

AIIB
 	
Energy Sector Strategy: Sustainable Energy for Asia
	S	2018	Guiding principles:
			• Promote energy access and security
			• Realize energy efficiency potential
			• Reduce the carbon intensity of energy supply
			• Local and regional pollution management
			• Catalyze private capital
			• Promote regional cooperation and connectivity
			   – Oil and coal-fired power plants would be considered if they replace existing less-efficient capacity or are essential to the reliability and integrity of the system, or if no viable or affordable alternative exists in specific cases
			   – Oil and natural gas processing, transportation, and distribution will be supported if they improve energy security or promote regional integration and trade

IsDB Energy Sector Policy	P	2018	Four policy pillars: • Increase access to modern energy services • Scale up renewable energy • Increase energy efficiency • Improve knowledge services

continued on next page

Table A1 *continued*

Energy Policy Key Publications	Policy/ Strategy/ Other	Year of Launch	Highlights and Position on Fossil Fuels
EIB Energy Lending Policy	P	2019	Four themes: • Unlocking energy efficiency • Decarbonizing energy supply • Supporting innovative technologies and new types of energy infrastructure • Securing the enabling infrastructure – EIB will not support (i) the production of oil and natural gas; (ii) traditional gas infrastructure (networks, storage, refining facilities); (iii) power generation technologies resulting in GHG emissions above 250 grams of CO_2 per kilowatt-hour of electricity generated, averaged over the lifetime for gas-fired power plants seeking to integrate low-carbon fuels; and (iv) large-scale heat production infrastructure based on unabated oil, natural gas, coal, or peat

EBRD
 	
Energy Sector Strategy 2019–2023
	S	2018	Four interrelated strategic directions:
			• Decarbonization and electrification
			• Well-functioning energy markets
			• Cleaner oil and gas value chains
			• Energy-efficient and inclusive economies
			  – No thermal coal mining or coal-fired electricity generation capacity
			  – No upstream oil exploration

Memorandum Green Economy Transition Approach 2021–2025 (July 2020)	O	2020	(…) (i) increase low-carbon energy supply from renewable energy and low-carbon fuels such as hydrogen; (ii) natural gas as a transition fuel; (…) financing activities will focus on innovative renewable energy systems and low-carbon fuel transportation and storage, utility-scale storage and the upgrade of gas and hydrogen transportation infrastructure
IADB Energy Sector Framework Document	O	2018	Thematic lines: • Energy access–coverage, quality, reliability, and affordability in the provision of energy services • Energy sustainability–energy efficiency, renewable energy, and climate change mitigation and adaptation, and reduction of environmental impacts in the long term • Energy security–energy infrastructure and regional energy integration for the provision of reliable services • Energy governance–institutions, regulation, policies, and information to foster the sector's long-term economic and financial sustainability – IADB will give a lower priority to fossil-fuel technologies, unless the investments make sense from an economic standpoint taking externalities into account, for example: in the rehabilitation of existing plants, substitution of solid or liquid fossil with cleaner gaseous fossil fuels; or to meet the demand for energy services.
Environmental and Social Policy Framework	O	2020	IADB will not finance: Activities that are inconsistent with IADB's commitments to address the challenges of climate change and promote environmental and social sustainability, such as: • Thermal coal mining or coal-fired power generation and associated facilities • Upstream oil exploration and development projects • Upstream gas exploration and development projects

continued on next page

Table A1 *continued*

Energy Policy Key Publications	Policy/ Strategy/ Other	Year of Launch	Highlights and Position on Fossil Fuels
WBG Energy Directions 2013	S	2013	Five directions: • Focus on Poor People – Universal Access • Accelerate Efficiency Gains • Expand Renewable Energy • Create an Enabling Environment • Intensify Global Advocacy – Greenfield coal-fired power in exceptional cases only

ADB = Asian Development Bank, AfDB = African Development Bank, AIIB = Asian Infrastructure Investment Bank, CO_2 = carbon dioxide, EBRD = European Bank for Reconstruction and Development, EIB = European Investment Bank, GHG = greenhouse gas, IADB = Inter-American Development Bank, IsDB = Islamic Development Bank, WBG = World Bank Group.

Source: Compiled by ADB.

Table A2: Links between the Guiding Principles of the Energy Policy and the Seven Operational Priorities of ADB Strategy 2030

Guiding Principles of Energy Policy	Support to Operational Priorities
1. Securing energy for a prosperous and inclusive Asia and the Pacific	OP1—Addressing remaining poverty and reducing inequalities: provision of access for power, light, clean cooking, and heating. OP2—Accelerating gender equality: reducing persistent gender gaps, addressing gender inequality, and reducing women's burden of care and unpaid work.
2. Building a sustainable and resilient energy future	OP3—Tackling climate change, building climate and disaster resilience, and enhancing environmental sustainability: through the increased use of renewable and low-carbon energy, achieve a planned and rapid phaseout of coal in Asia and the Pacific. OP4—Making cities more livable: energy efficiency, renewable energy, and electric mobility will help make cities more livable by improving ambient air quality. OP5—Promoting rural development and food security: off-grid electrification and solar pumps to support agricultural activities that enhance food security in rural communities.
3. Engaging with institutions and framing policy reforms	OP6—Strengthening governance and institutional capacity: support energy sector reforms, including strengthened regulatory frameworks and introduction of competitive markets; attract private sector investment; and achieve the long-term financial sustainability of energy entities by ensuring the financial viability of investments and the maintenance of infrastructure assets.
4. Promoting regional cooperation to enhance energy security	OP7—Foster regional cooperation and integration: promote regional cooperation through policy dialogue, knowledge sharing, and investments in cross-border energy trading to reduce greenhouse gas emissions and increase energy security.
5. Providing integrated solutions and cross-sector operations to maximize development impact	Supporting all seven OPs through integrated energy and cross-sector solutions to address more complex development challenges.

OP = operational priority.

Source: Asian Development Bank.